About This Workbook

So you want to be in business for yourself. What an exciting opportunity to start a new venture from nothing and watch it grow into a profitable company. Originally written in 2009 for a professor at a HBCU - Historically Black College or University – as a supplemental resource in a business course, *Entrepreneurship 101: The New Reality of Business Ownership* is finally available for all would-be entrepreneurs with a passion to own your business. Stop delaying the dream! In this economically and politically charged environment, it is even more critical for young adults, particularly in the Communities of Color around the globe, to forge a path to build sustained wealth, lift each other up through encouraging collaborative efforts that support complex enterprises. This workbook is not for young adults only. There are many in each generational category who aspire to start businesses. Expand your networks to be inclusive and diverse.

This highly-interactive, practical and easy to understand workbook will walk you through each step of the process using the 4 P's to success --- Passion, Preparation, Planning and Persistence. The attempt was to make the business planning part less challenging so that you can be better prepared for what develops next. As you approach each section, take the time to complete the exercises and worksheets with as much detail as possible. Gather your **trusted** friends and partners to take the journey with you. I suggest that you not do this alone, for there is strength in numbers. However, be cautious of who you include in your circle of influence; hopefully these are people you value and support your efforts. Once completed, the entire workbook will become a reference resource to return to as your business grows. Whether you are selling a product or providing a service, the set-by-step instructions will be fun and exciting as you literally watch your plan become a reality.

Are you ready? Let's start a business --- **NOW!**

A special thank you to Ted Haenlein, Finance Instructor, University of Phoenix, Richmond – Virginia Beach campus for his review and critique of the manuscript.

TABLE OF CONTENTS

TABLE OF CONTENTS

TABLE OF CONTENTS

The 4Ps of Entrepreneurship

Business owner or entrepreneur or as most recently referred to as a solopreneur. Regardless of which term you use, the outcome of the definition is still the same. According to Webster's dictionary, the term entrepreneur was derived from the old French word *entreprendre,* which means to undertake. The listing goes on the further define the word as "one who organizes, manages, and assumes the risks of a business or enterprise."

Before you read any further, take a few moments to focus on a few key words that will help you determine if business ownership is right for you. First, are you *organized*? Having excellent organization skills are definitely an asset when there are various papers to file, plans to write, forms to complete, customers to call, employees to pay, schedules to keep and other activities too numerous to count. Being organized is critical for a business owner. Of course you can partner or hire someone who is organized.

Next, how are your management skills? Can you make hard decisions, oversee projects and motivate employees? How about resolve conflicts and analyze data? Being a good manager is also part of being a successful business owner.

Finally, are you a risk taker? Are there degrees of risk that you are comfortable assuming? If so, how much risk are you willing to take with your money, borrowed money or invested money? Many times, entrepreneurs have to predict outcomes and forecast probabilities based on nothing more than research.

Yes, there are a lot of good reasons to own your own business and start-up can be an exciting time for budding entrepreneurs. But to succeed, business owners must be prepared to assume the majority, if not all of responsibility for the business and anyone else who will be affected by the decisions he/she makes. With this definition firmly in mind, do you have what it takes to be a successful business owner?

The "P" Factor – Passion, Preparation, Planning and Persistence

As you move through this workbook, notice that each section introduces one of four critical components of business development --- Passion, Preparation, Planning and Persistence. Take extra care to focus on how the "P" factor can increase the probability of success, as you complete each exercise/worksheet.

Section 1 – Finding Your Passion   Section II – Preparing for Business Ownership

Section III - Planning for Success   Section IV – Persistence is Key

SECTION I

FINDING
YOUR PASSION

The Right Stuff

Let's face it. The thought of being in business for yourself sounds pretty good, right? You can work when you want and sleep late every day, with no nagging boss to tell you what to do. Oh and by the way, you will make lots and lots of money because everyone will want your product or service. Sounds wonderful, right?

Now, stop daydreaming! It's time for a reality check. Many individuals fantasize about becoming an entrepreneur, especially those who have had less than positive corporate experiences or have been recently downsized. But business ownership is not a fantasy. It takes hard work and many hours of dedication. Successful business owners are passionate about what they do and they have to be. Why? Because an entrepreneur is not just the owner of the business, but he/she is the owner, salesperson, marketer and in some cases manufacturer or service provider. They are the negotiators, customer service representatives and the complaint department. In some cases, they even handle technology needs.

A budding entrepreneur must be prepared to handle all aspects of the business. He/she must possess both the necessary interpersonal and professional skills to succeed. Before jumping in to business ownership, answer and score the questions below to determine whether you have *the right stuff.*

REALITY CHECK

Starting a business takes courage and commitment. You will work harder than you have ever worked in your life. If you are truly passionate about being an entrepreneur, the reward of owning your business is well worth the energy.

The Right Stuff

Do you have the RIGHT STUFF?

1.	Are you independent?	Y ___ N ___
2.	Are you a positive thinker?	Y ___ N ___
3.	Are you an overachiever?	Y ___ N ___
4.	Are you assertive?	Y ___ N ___
5.	Are you afraid of making decisions?	Y ___ N ___
6.	Do you have good social skills?	Y ___ N ___
7.	Do you say what you mean?	Y ___ N ___
8.	Can people count on you? Are you responsible?	Y ___ N ___
9.	Are you a good listener?	Y ___ N ___
10.	Do you see yourself putting in 16 hours a day on your business?	Y ___ N ___
11.	Do you have problem solving strengths?	Y ___ N ___
12.	Do you have a take-charge attitude?	Y ___ N ___
13.	Can you multi-task?	Y ___ N ___
14.	Are you good with money --- can you budget?	
15.	Are you a risk taker?	

Your Score = Y _____   Your Score = N _____

Give yourself one (1) point for each answer.

If your total "Y" scores are in the 13-15 range, you have the Right Stuff and should do well as an entrepreneur.

If your total "Y" scores are in the 10-13 range, you may be a successful business owner if you focus on improving your weak areas and extra hard on achieving your clearly defined goals.

If your total "Y" scores are lower that 10 or your total "N" scores are higher overall, you may want to re-examine your choice to be a business owner.

Another useful tool is the DISC assessment available online for $25.

Defining Your Business

For those of you who have the *right stuff*, starting and running a business should bring fulfillment and satisfaction. However, just wanting to be a business owner or entrepreneur is not enough to be successful. Now you have to determine what type of business you want to own and whether the market supports the product or service you will be selling. This requires that you know you the industry that your business will operate in extremely well.

Having completed the self-assessment in the previous chapter, you should now have a better understanding of your strengths and weaknesses, your best skills and the types of activities that drive your passion. Armed with this information, start to think about the type of business that will support your strengths and allow you to do things that bring you fulfillment and joy.

For example, if you enjoy cooking, you might think about opening a restaurant or starting a catering business. If you like gardening, how about starting a lawn and garden service or a flower shop. For those that enjoy taking care of others, maybe opening a home health company that provides various types of medical services to homebound individuals or seniors. Or maybe you want to produce music for up and coming artists, open a workout facility or start a financial planning service. The options and opportunities are limitless once you identify the type of business that will compliment your personality.

You will have to name your business. Choosing a name for your business is one of the most important tasks in the business start-up process.

Characteristics of a Good Business Name

- Memorable and easily recognizable (called **brandable**)
- Easy to pronounce and spell
- Perhaps unique for your industry
- Must have an available dot.com or .org address for online marketing

It is critical that you invest the time necessary to ensure a wise naming choice. Brainstorm with your support team and/or hold mini-focus groups to gauge the response from would be customers.

Defining Your Business

There are several structures you can consider for your business. Please conduct the proper research, review the advantages of each to select which is best for you. The primary types of entities are sole proprietorship, partnership, S or C Corporation, or Limited Liability Company or LLC. More importantly, contemplate such factors are liability, tax benefits and raising capital. Remember not to leave your personal assets vulnerable or exposed to business creditors.

Complete the worksheets and exercises on the following page by answering the questions. Keep in mind the results of your self-assessment. Answer the questions in as much detail as possible.

If you could own a business, what would it be? Make a list of all the possible options you are considering.

Business Type	Why did you choose this business?	Advantages	Disadvantages

What distinguishes your service or product from other like offerings on the market?

_____

_____

_____

_____

Who are your customers?

_____

_____

_____

_____

_____

Defining Your Business

If you are sharing your business with partners, identify who these partners will be --- family members, friends or co-workers. Do these partners understand your vision for the business and do they share the same goals? What are their strengths and weaknesses? What agreements should you have in place to protect your and their investments in the business?

_____

_____

_____

_____

_____

_____

If your venture is NOT a home-based business, where do you want it to be located? Why?

_____

_____

_____

_____

_____

_____

_____

_____

_____

_____

_____

Will you use a business coach to assist you in the start-up process? If so, who might that be?

_____

_____

Defining Your Business

Your 60-Second Commercial

Pretend you are addressing the Shark Tank celebrities or a venture capitalist (VC). In 60 seconds or less you should be able to communicate who you are, what type of business you have and how it would benefit your targeted customers. The template below will assist you in developing your commercial.

My name is _____ and I am the owner of

_____

_____

.

Our business (tell the what your business does) _____

_____

_____

_____

_____

Our customers (identify your customers and communicate how they benefit from your product or service)

_____

_____

_____

The Close: Ask the listener if he/she would like more information about your product or service._____

_____

_____

Defining Your Business

Naming Your Business

Brainstorm possible business names and prioritize your choices. Say the names aloud to hear how each sounds. Ask others for feedback and select the best responses.

Potential Business Name	Why Chosen	Initial response from others

Why New Businesses Fail

Did you know that approximately 50% of all new businesses fail within the first five years? That is the estimate given by the U.S. Small Business Administration, the federal agency charged with assisting and counseling small and potential small business owners. With this knowledge, what can a new business owner do to ensure success? Luckily, there have been many studies on small business successes and failures over the past few years that have identified many of the pitfalls new business owners should avoid. Spinning those study results to reflect positive results, each new business owner must identify key success factors for his/her particular venture.

What are key success factors? Key success factors (KSFs) are the benchmarks by which you will define and measure whether or not your business is meeting the desired goals. Think of it like this --- without key success factors how will you know if you are doing the right things to be successful? How will you know when to change course and try something different? Without these key success indicators, business owners make costly mistakes that could ultimately cause the venture to fail.

So how do you define success? Here is where your knowledge of both your company's service or product and industry comes in to play. Think about all the activities that you might do as a business owner of this type of venture that if done well, will ensure that your business meets its goals successfully.

Let's look at an example of key success factors for a small cleaning company. Here is what we know about the company and the industry:

Company:	New, start-up capital $5000
Industry:	Highly competitive
Niche:	Green cleaning
Industry Experience:	Little
Business Skills:	Strong

KEY SUCCESS FACTORS (KSF) FOR MIKE'S CLEANING SERVICE

1 – Hire committed, qualified cleaners with a positive attitude and train them well.
2 – Provide exceptional customer service to customers with a service guarantee model.
3 – Communicate expectations to workers and pay them accordingly.
4 – Identify and expand on niche to stay ahead of the competition.
5 – Retain dedicated, long-term customers by offering extra incentives.
6 – Introduce new/additional product or service to bring value-added opportunity.
7 – Expenses must not exceed start-up capital for initial 12 months; no outside loans.
8 – Company ROI must exceed 25% of start-up within 12 months.

Why New Businesses Fail

These are a few examples of key success factors for a small cleaning service. Notice that Mike's Cleaning Service defined success based on his knowledge of the cleaning industry and what it would take to be competitive. All business owners must be able to identify key indicators that drive the success of the company. What are your KSFs? Using the worksheet below, identify the KSFs for your company and define the success measures.

Can you list other reasons why businesses fail?

More statistics...nine out of ten companies operating today will eventually fail. One in three new businesses fails within six months. Identifying key success factors are mandatory to ensure company viability.

Why New Businesses Fail
Defining Your Key Success Factors

KEY SUCCESS FACTOR	MEASURED HOW?

Business Start-ups in Today's Economy

More so than ever before, small business owners have created between 60 and 80 percent of new jobs. There are over 20 million small businesses that produce about 39% of the nation's gross national product. Small businesses represent 99.7% of all employers and will continue to be a powerful economic force in the years ahead in spite of recent negative financial events. These businesses will outnumber major corporations as more workers leave to establish a path of self-sufficiency towards entrepreneurship. Entrepreneurship is a major contributor to our nation's well-being in terms of economic growth and new job creation.

In the Global Entrepreneurship Monitor (GEM) research conducted by Babson College, London School of Business and the Kaufmann Foundation, six key factors were recognized to identify the differences in entrepreneurial cultures in 10 countries. These are: the level of perceived entrepreneurial opportunity; entrepreneurial capacity or the motivation and skill to take advantage of the opportunity; infrastructure, broadly defined as the availability of financing, land, facilities, employees, suppliers, government assistance, utility costs, transportation, tax concessions, etc.; the demographic make-up of the population, including age, gender and population growth; education; and, culture, particularly the expectations and participation of women in new business start-ups, the acceptance within a country of differences in the level of income among individuals, and the respect for start-ups. (09Ja)

A small business is a company operating with less than 500 employees. Of 112.4 million nonfarm private sector workers in 2002, small firms with fewer than 500 workers employed 56.4 million and large firms, 56.0 million. Smaller firms with fewer than 100 employees employed 40.5 million. Two-thirds of new businesses started will survive the first two years. Forty-four percent will survive at least four years. (Small Business Administration)

SECTION II

PREPARING FOR BUSINESS OWNERSHIP

Personal and Family Considerations

As with anything worth having, starting a business requires sacrifices from the business owner and anyone else associated with the business. This is why it is suggested that potential entrepreneurs discuss the impact business ownership will have on their family, friends and significant others. Your *team* must provide the support and buy-in you will need to be successful going forward.

The first component of the preparation stage begins with identifying and gathering together all those that your business decision will touch to discuss your ideas and concerns. Do not make the mistake of thinking that you can go it alone. You will need a support team to encourage you, provide emotional support, keep you grounded, balanced and on track to meet your business goals.

Starting a business can be exciting and stressful at the same time. Ensure that those on your support team understand why you are passionate about your product or service. Communicate your vision with them and update them regularly as you move toward your goal.

Topics to Discuss with Your Support Team

- Time constraints – balancing work and home life
- Weekend and late night hours
- Home-based business versus alternate location
- Financial considerations (more in next topic area)
- Family members as co-owners
- Working part-time while you grow the business
- Working full-time while you grow the business

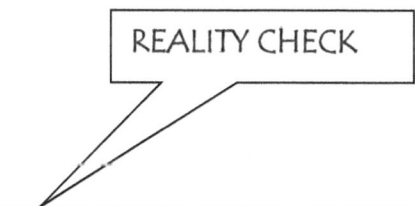

REALITY CHECK

While it may not be apparent now, your support team will provide the necessary encouragement to keep you going, when things get tough. Choose carefully.

Personal and Family Considerations

What are your goals? How will these goals align with your "life goals"? (Intangible, broad statements of what you wish to accomplish with your business)

_____

_____

_____

_____

_____

Define your vision that you wish to communicate with your support team. What are the values that you wish for your support team to endorse?

_____

_____

_____

_____

_____

_____

_____

_____

Identify an objective (tangible actions) for each business goal listed above.

_____

_____

_____

_____

_____

_____

_____

_____

Personal and Family Considerations

Who are the members of your support team?

_____

_____

_____

_____

_____

_____

Ministerial /Spiritual Team		**Family & Friends**

You, The Business Owner

Professional & Business Team Members

Financial Planning
Show Me the Money!

One of the main reasons that business fail is due to inadequate start-up capital. In other words --- show me the money! Armed with a wonderful idea, a motivating vision and $$$$, budding entrepreneurs jump feet first into the process of starting a business. However, at the time many do not realize that the process may take much longer that intended before they see a return on their investment (ROI) dollars.

Decisions about how and with what money your business will be financed must be determined early in the start-up planning. It is critical to define how much money you will need to meet your goals and objectives. In addition, business owners have to decide if their initial funding source will be entirely from personal dollars or borrowed from investors. Each source has its advantages and disadvantages, giving the business owner something to think about.

FUNDING SOURCE	ADVANTAGES	DISADVANTAGES
Self-funded personal savings and/or 401K	Nothing to pay back. There could be franchise aligned advantages.	Not an unlimited pool of dollars in case of an emergency
Family-funded	Business stays in the family; little paperwork involved.	Family members may wish to have a say in the day-to-day operations; trust factor.
Friend-funded	May be an easier sell especially if this is someone that you trust.	Same as above but may wish to be a formal investor.
Bank or formal lending institution	Direct and straightforward transaction.	Must convince loan officer of business viability; may need collateral and interest rates may not be negotiable
Private investor funding – Angel Network, Small Business Loans, Venture Capitalist, Federal and state programs, etc.	If you have a good product or service and a good business plan, you may obtain a loan for the entire amount needed.	You will owe someone or an entity; you must meet a predetermined payment schedule; less negotiation on interest rates for ROI.

Another very important factor funding sources consider is your knowledge of the business and your ability to run a business successfully. This determines the level of risk that the source is willing to take in loaning you the money. This is especially true for new or start-up businesses because the company has no history of profitability.

Financial Planning
Show Me the Money!

Once your business plan is completed (Section III) you will be in a better position to shop for funding whether from personal, private or public sources. Remember, it is better to have too much money than not enough. Make sure that you are clear on how much money you will need, before you approach potential lenders.

Financing Your Business

Identify possible sources of initial start-up funding for your business

_____

_____

_____

If you are planning to self-fund your business, how long can you live without paying yourself a salary? It could be a minimum of 12 months for most businesses or up to five years for brick and mortar.

_____

_____

How is your personal credit history? Is your credit score at least 680?

_____

_____

Will revenue from this business be your sole source of income for you and/or your family?

_____

_____

_____

Do you have a bank account and/or a relationship with a local financial institution you have used in the past?

_____

_____

_____

Financial Planning
Show Me the Money!

Financing Your Business

Research alternative funding resources before shopping your business plan to ensure the best possible deal.

POSSIBLE FUNDING SOURCES	CONTACT INFO	POSSIBLE OFFER	Y/N

REALITY CHECK

Check out online sources for funding as part of your research. There are quite a few legitimate networks of funders willing to work with new business owners. For example, http://www.gobignetwork.com/funding/

Ongoing Research

One of the first things that you will *learn* as a new business owner is that the *learning* never ends. In today's economy the market changes rapidly and the buying public responds just as quickly. As a business owner, you have to stay abreast of any changes in your industry that may affect sales.

For a new business, ongoing research is a major component of the process. The more you know about every facet of owning a business, the more likely you are to be successful. Information to assist entrepreneurs is available much more readily than in years past. With the internet at your fingertips, business owners have an infinite pool of resource material from which to tap twenty-four hours a day.

Return to this page as you work through the rest of this workbook. Use it to jump-start your research when you begin implementing your business plan.

FUNDING OPTIONS

    Contact your local Small Business Administration (SBA - **https://www.sba.gov/**)

    Loans: Small Business Development Centers (SBDC)
                Online Lending Centers
                Venture Capitalists
                Federal qualifying lenders (SBA)
                Banks

GENERAL BUSINESS START-UP SUPPORT

    Small Business Administration
    SCORE – Retired entrepreneurs that offer free advice to small businesses
        (**www.score.org**)

ONLINE NEWS

    Wall Street Journal
    Community, local and state papers

COMMUNITY & CIVIC ORGANIZATIONS

    Local Chamber of Commerce

INTERNET

    Crowd funding sources such as Kickstarter, Indiegogo, RocketHub and Grow Venture Community, are a few places to start.

SECTION III

PLANNING FOR SUCCESS

What is a Business Plan?

Whether referred to as a blueprint, roadmap or recipe for success, a business plan is a valuable tool to use as a barometer to build and monitor your business. Anyone who expects to expend a significant amount of time and energy on starting a business that generates some source of profit and income would be well advised to put it in writing.

Business plans are also advisable when seeking financial assistance to start, maintain and grow your venture. Banks, venture capitalists and other financial institutions require that you present this plan to access their resources. A suggested business plan outline could include the following components.

1. Cover Sheet

2. Executive Summary

3. Company Description

4. Management and Operating Structure

5. Market Analysis

6. Sales/Marketing

7. Financial Plan and Forecasts

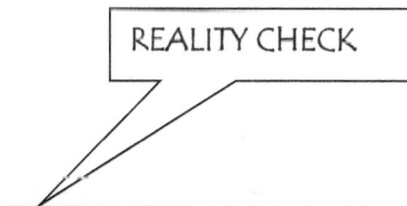

REALITY CHECK

Your business plan is a working document that communicates, manages and helps you plan for the future. Become familiar with it and be ready to make adjustments as needed.

Practicality versus Reality

Launching a new business is scary, challenging at best and requires patience, commitment and follow-through. Lots of follow-through! There are a thousand ideas and dreams that would be entrepreneurs have died from lack of trying. So why do statistics show the steady growth of new small businesses every year? Opportunities abound for small business owners especially with the use of new technology and global access to a worldwide marketplace. As long as people continue to dream and aspire to become business owners, there are those who will try, those who will succeed, and those who will fail and try again. For example, there is the success story of the former governor of a southern state who failed twice before hitting the bull's eye in the cellular phone market. Consequently, he became a millionaire.

However, you would be well advised to perform due diligence before hanging out the "open for business" shingle. What does this involve? Using this workbook has already started you on the path to evaluate if this is the right time, right idea and right place for you to move forward. Even the best ideas can fail miserably if you do not have a plan. As you proceed on this journey, take some time to acquaint yourself with strong principles to guide you throughout your path to success.

There are some business experts who may suggest that spending valuable time writing a business plan is wasteful unless you are seeking funding from a financial institution. If this is the case, the financial officer will ask to see your business plan. Having or not having a plan does not guarantee success; however, it still has its merits as a useful tool.

Think about it. How do you intend to use your business plan? Who are your customers? Explain here.

_____

_____

_____

_____

_____

_____

_____

_____

_____

Essential Components of a Business Plan

Cover Sheet

The cover sheet simply identifies the name of the business, address, telephone number and website. It can also include a non-disclosure or confidentiality statement to protect the business owner(s).

Executive Summary

Within the overall outline of the business plan, the executive summary will follow the title or cover page and is generally written last. The summary should tell the reader what you want. This is very important to address up front so the reader is not left guessing. Clearly state what you are asking for in the summary. It should capture your reader's attention and generate interest in your product or service.

The summary statement should be kept short and businesslike, probably no more than half a page. It could be longer, depending on how complicated the use of funds may be, but the summary of a business plan, like the summary of a loan application, is generally no longer than one page. Within that space, you will need to provide a summary of your entire business plan.

EXAMPLE 1.0

The Cookie Store, LLC is a start-up bakery located in Chesterfield, Virginia and was founded to provide the most wholesome, nutritious and delicious sweet potato based products such as cookies, muffins, pastries, cakes and spreads. It began initially as a home baked business for friends, family and local businesses. The sweet potato cookies were baked and sold in a popular local supermarket chain and featured in the local newspaper. Shortly thereafter, the owners decided to assist with the formulation of the recipe for mass production.

The company plans to capitalize on the strong market for natural, wholesome and more health oriented products as evidenced by the public's demand for healthier food products that taste good. The Cookie Store, LLC plans to capture the local market and enter the local grocery store chain, provide frozen dough products for fund raiser (or boxed items for sale), establish an Internet order website and develop an international presence.

The Cookie Store aims to provide its products at a competitive price to meet the demand of middle-to-higher income markets and consumers.

Company Description

The company description or background should provide a general overview of your business. It describes the business you are starting, how it came to be, where it is today and what is expected in the future. When defining the nature of the business, look at the market's needs and how the business expects to satisfy those needs. The company description should not be any longer than a few pages.

This section should accomplish two things. First, develop a statement describing how your business came to exist and illustrate your personal circumstances that brought you to this business opportunity. This adds a personal touch especially if it has a human interest element. Second, summarize the information you will be covering in the company description section.

EXAMPLE 1.1

The company plans to capitalize on the strong market for natural, wholesome and more health oriented products as evidenced by the public's demand for healthier food products that taste good. The Cookie Store, LLC plans to capture the local market and enter the local grocery store chain, provide frozen dough products for fund raiser (or boxed items for sale), establish an Internet order website and develop an international presence.

In the space below, begin writing your company description.

_____

_____

_____

_____

_____

_____

_____

_____

_____

_____

_____

Management and Operating Structure

Are you ready to start thinking about how you are going to manage your business? You will need to include details about your management, organizational and ownership structure. Your business plan provides information about your management's ability to guide the business and its functionality with clear lines of responsibilities. Even if you are the only employee, your plan should include information that will assure the potential investors that accountability for the business' success has been well thought out.

Organizational structure and ownership of the business are important for start-ups. Here is where business owners make substantial use of multi-tasking skills and wearing many hats. Many new business owners have extensive backgrounds from former employment experiences and bring this knowledge with them. However, business owners would be prudent to highlight some uniqueness, special skills or qualities that demonstrate the business savvy needed to manage and market your business services or products.

Resumes, biographies and acknowledgements of certifications, awards, publications and other notable accomplishments should be listed in the appendix or as attachments of your business plan. These documents further support the capabilities of the management and principals running the business.

Operating Structure

Business owners have options when it comes to deciding what legal entity works best for managing the venture. Choose wisely. The most commonly used operating structures are:

Sole proprietorship – single owner
Partnership – two or more persons in business together
Corporation – more complex and requires filing incorporation papers
Limited Liability Corporation LLC) - provides advantages of both a corporation and partnership structure, but is easier to operate

Limited Liability Company (LLC) is frequently used type of hybrid business structure that more start-ups use to form their ventures because it protects the owner's personal assets from any business liabilities.

Organizational Structure

Who reports to whom? That is what an organizational structure identifies. Unless you are the only owner --- a sole proprietorship --- your business will have other employees. The positions and titles of these employees define your organizational structure. In smaller businesses

In communicating the organizational structure of your business, something as simple as a chart defining the roles and responsibilities would suffice with any number of employees. As the company grows, this chart can be flexible to show more functional areas to assure that nothing is left to chance and that there is a system of checks and balances in the business. This is important for investors to see, for your employees to understand and for your customers are comfortable knowing you can handle their needs.

The two owners of The Cookie Store, LLC, James and Denise, have distinct roles in the business. Their ownership ratio is 51/49. A simple organization chart shows the following.

EXAMPLE 1.2

Identify the important positions you need to fill in your business in the following organization chart. Two key roles that must be clearly differentiated:

1 – Who will produce/deliver the product or service?
2 – Who will manage the daily operations not related to the product/service production and delivery?

Draw additional boxes as needed.

Market Analysis

You have a product or service that you wish to sell, but how do you know who to sell it to or whether or not someone --- anyone --- wants to buy it? This is what marketing is all about. A business owner must determine who their potential customers are and what a potential customer wants or needs, then find a way to meet these needs. This is the first step in performing a market analysis. All successful business owners must direct their efforts on ensuring that they are meeting the expectations of their customers.

In addition, business owners must understand the importance of trust in marketing their products or services. People buy from companies that not only meet their needs, but also from companies that they perceive are honest and trustworthy. Building a *relationship* with a potential customer increases the probability that they will patronize your service or use your product. Therefore, trust is a major component of the marketing process.

Marketing your product or service is an important aspect of a new business, to ensure continued success as the business grows.

Performing a Marketing Analysis

When performing a marketing analysis, reference the information gathered during your early research. This data would include in-depth research of the business industry type, the target market, the product/service offering, market trends, and growth projections and of course research about the competition.

Let's review each focus area of a marketing analysis.

Focus Area I: SWOT Analysis

A SWOT (strengths, weaknesses, opportunities, threats) analysis is the first step in the marketing process that assists the business owner in identifying and focusing on key issues that will affect the success of the organization. Used as an assessment tool, the result of the analysis assists the business owner in identifying underlying factors that may affect the growth of the business. Divided into four distinct components, the strengths and weaknesses area of the tool evaluates the internal workings of a company, many of which were identified in Section II of this workbook. The opportunities and threats data is obtained from information gathered from external research including market trends, economic forecasts, and target market and competitor data. This will be covered in the next section.

Begin a SWOT analysis for your company by completing the blocks below with information gathered in Section II and other internal researched resources. As you move forward in the workbook, return to the SWOT analysis to update it with information gathered from external research.

Focus Area I: SWOT Analysis

Strengths

- List and prioritize all of your qualifications and resources that will make your service or product better than your competitors, i.e. immediate marketable need, unique product/service, subject matter expertise.

_____

_____

_____

_____

_____

_____

_____

_____

_____

_____

- Next Steps – Identify how you will leverage your company's strengths to increase profitability.

_____

_____

_____

_____

_____

_____

_____

_____

_____

Focus Area I: SWOT Analysis

Weaknesses

- List and prioritize any attribute that presents an obstacle to the success of the business, i.e. financial resources, lack of business management strengths, availability of trained workers.

_____

_____

_____

_____

_____

_____

_____

_____

_____

- Next Steps – Identify how you will either correct these weaknesses, perceived or real or turn them in to a positive advantage.

_____

_____

_____

_____

_____

_____

_____

_____

_____

Focus Area I: SWOT Analysis

Opportunities

- List and prioritize any known or perceived advantages that could improve your competitive position, i.e. first business in the area offering this service or selling this product, a patented methodology for this service, target market is growing for this specialty area.

_____

_____

_____

_____

_____

_____

_____

_____

_____

- Next Steps – Identify how you will leverage these opportunities to generate profit for the company and increase the likelihood for success.

_____

_____

_____

_____

_____

_____

_____

_____

_____

Focus Area I: SWOT Analysis

Threats

- List and prioritize any known or perceived potential risk/negative consequence that could diminish the success or your business, i.e. layoff in areas that affect your target market, new tax legislation that will significantly lower your profit margin, new competitor with similar specialty product may absorb sales.

_____

_____

_____

_____

_____

_____

_____

_____

- Next Steps – Addressing any threats require immediate and decisive action. Identify how and when you will make corrective action in this area.

_____

_____

_____

_____

_____

_____

_____

_____

Focus Area II: Product/Service Offering

Describe your product or service in as much detail as possible, identifying those features that you feel are unique selling points for your venture. Make sure that you write in easy to understand words --- no flowery or show-off words. Remember, you want the reader to feel your passion for this venture and feel that he/she can trust the product or service you are providing.

Ensure that you include any additional or value-added services you provide before or after the sale. For example, do you provide follow-up maintenance questions free of charge for the next 30 days, or telephone coaching or discounts for purchasing additional services? Business owners should be able to clearly communicate both verbally and in writing, a concise description of the service or product.

- Write a detailed description of the product or service that you will provide.

_____

_____

_____

_____

_____

_____

_____

_____

_____

_____

_____

_____

_____

Focus Area III: Market Trends

Purple tie-dyed shirts, hybrid cars, patent leather platform shoes and mega churches are examples of market trends and fads. Can you tell which item falls in what category? Identifying and understanding the difference between the two is key to successfully marketing your service or product.

Defining a trend

When defining market trends, business owners identify a direction, slant or tendency of a particular course of action. It is a movement toward a way of thinking that links the buying public to a specific item. In the example above, the purchasing of a hybrid car falls into the trend category. In 2006 - 2007, consumers began to focus on preserving the earth. Living "green" became a trend that forced companies to change their way of doing business and marketers to develop new ways to capitalize or sell that change. The result has been a boom in "green everything" from restaurants to shoes, cleaning services to construction. The trend has no definitive end in sight, providing unlimited new opportunities for green business expansion in every industry.

By contrast purple tie-dyed shirts and patent leather platform shoes fall in the fad category. The difference is in the longevity or duration of the product or service and whether it has a long-term effect on the market. The lifespan of a fad is much shorter than a trend. Fads may come and go over a period of time but a trend tends to change an industry and can present a sustainable investment opportunity.

Define your product or service again. Now, is it a fad or a trend? Explain and give supporting research for your answer.

_____

_____

_____

_____

_____

_____

_____

_____

Focus Area III: Market Trends

Identify **social, environmental or legislative trends** that may impact how your business is marketed, sold, perceived or changes the way the business operates.

_____

_____

_____

_____

_____

_____

Identify **technological trends** that may impact how your business is marketed, sold, perceived or changes the way the business operates.

_____

_____

_____

_____

_____

_____

_____

Identify **demographic trends** (age, ethnicity, income level, sexual orientation, occupation, marital status, etc.) that may impact how your business is marketed, sold, perceived or changes the way the business operates.

_____

_____

_____

_____

_____

_____

_____

Focus Area IV: Industry Analysis

In this section of your marketing plan, refer again to the research you completed in Section II of this workbook. What did you learn or discover about the industry that supports your business? Relate this information to the current marketing trends for your venture, to determine the health or survivability of your product or service. For example, is your particular industry experiencing a growth spurt or a decline in the market? What is the long-term and short-term forecast for the current market behavior?

It is critical that business owners stay abreast and ahead of current and predicted market forecasts, to accurately respond to the changing landscape of their particular industry. Complete the information on the following pages to facilitate an analysis of your industry.

Economic Forecast

Define the current economic outlook for your particular business, according to the following geographic areas and what, if any impact it may have on your business. Give careful consideration to workforce and employment rates, which drive income levels for your area and your target customers.

- Local community, city and/or state economic forecast

_____

_____

_____

_____

_____

_____

_____

_____

_____

Focus Area IV: Industry Analysis

- Regional economic forecast

_____
_____
_____
_____
_____
_____
_____
_____
_____
_____

- Nationwide forecast

_____
_____
_____
_____
_____
_____
_____
_____
_____
_____
_____
_____
_____
_____

Focus Area IV: Industry Analysis

- Global economic forecast

_____

_____

_____

_____

_____

Focus Area IV: Industry Analysis

Target Market

Can you identify your target market? These are your customers, the people who will purchase your product or use your services. Who are they and how do you find them? Go back to your earlier research and identify resources that can assist you in developing a profile of your potential customer. Once again, it is critical to clearly define these individuals as the target consumers that you will spend your time and money to attract.

Let's brainstorm!

- Describe the type of individuals, organizations or even other businesses that you expect will benefit from your product or service. Give supporting research for why you think this individual/entity is in your target market. List as many characteristics as possible, including the location of potential customers and their financial strength.

_____

_____

_____

_____

_____

_____

_____

_____

_____

CUSTOMER PROFILE MARKET SEGMENTATION

CATEGORY	CHARACTERISTICS	COMMENTS/ OBSERVATIONS
Income bracket		
Gender		
Age		
Ethnicity		
Family make-up		
Education level		
Lifestyle		
Health		
Occupation		
Religion		
Home ownership or renter		
Hobbies		
Geographic location		
Pet (s)		
Buying habits/motivation		
Live alone		
Organization - size		
Organization - type		
Organization – location		
Other		
Other		
Other		
Other		

Focus Area V: Competitive Advantage

Almost all businesses have some form of competition. Think about the services that you use or products that you purchase. Were there alternatives --- either direct or indirect--- that you could have utilized that would have met your needs? Did those services appeal to you? Now, think carefully about the service or products that you wish to sell to your target market. Are there other businesses that your customers can patronize that will appeal to their needs? Who are those businesses and are your offerings better than theirs?

These are the types of questions that business owners ask themselves in defining a competitive advantage for their product or service. Once identified, an owner should be able to clearly communicate why a customer should choose his or her business over another. This is called having a **competitive advantage** and businesses use it to drive potential customers to their business and away from their competitors.

There are four important steps in identifying your company's competitive advantage that can be easily remembered by *just keeping it* **R.E.A.L.** -

R - Research and thoroughly understand the major companies in your industry
E - Evaluate the competitor's business model and understand "how" they do business
A - Ask for information on specific products or services by posing as a customer.
L - List unique or distinguishing characteristics of your business --- your **niche** --- that you regard as different from the identified competitors and other like businesses

Once you have completed the steps in the R.E. A. L. model above, perform a comparative analysis of your business and your competitors. Determine each company's strengths and weaknesses and consider how you will address each to leverage your competitive advantage. Remember, customers buy from people that they trust, therefore factor customer perception into your comparison.

An ongoing analysis of the market should be a regular component of growing your business. The market changes rapidly and staying ahead of your competitors will increase your prospect for success.

The following exercises should assist you in defining your businesses' competitive advantage.

Focus Area V: Competitive Advantage

Following the R.E.A.L. model, complete the following information on your company's tops six (6) competitors.

COMPETITIVE ANALYSIS EXERCISE

Name/ Analysis	Competitor #1	Competitor #2	Competitor #3
Product/service type			
Promotion, selling/advertising strategies			
Target market			
Location/Facility Convenience and atmosphere			
Pricing			
Service Quality			
Niche/unique offerings			
Overall strengths			
Weaknesses			
Other			

COMPETITIVE ANALYSIS EXERCISE

Name/ Analysis	Competitor #4	Competitor #5	Competitor #6
Product/service type			
Promotion, selling/advertising strategies			
Target market			
Location/Facility convenience and atmosphere			
Pricing			
Service Quality			
Niche/unique offering			
Overall strengths			
Weaknesses			
Other			
Other			

Focus Area V: Competitive Advantage

In the worksheet below, prioritize your competitors based on the information gathered and summarize the findings. Compare each competitor's strength and weakness with the list that you developed in step four of the R.E.A.L. model. Review how your business measures up with the top six and address any disparities or concerns with a recommendation for corrective action. Likewise, address how to leverage your strengths to attract your desired target market.

SUMMARY	STRENGTHS	WEAKNESSES	MY COMPANY RECOMMENDATIONS
Competitor #1			
Competitor #2			
Competitor #3			
Competitor #4			
Competitor #5			
Competitor #6			

Marketing/Sales Strategy

To get customers to buy from a business, business owners must create awareness that you exist and have something your target market needs. This is part of your marketing/ sales strategy. Your customers are the lifeblood of the business, providing you with the cash receipts or income needed to grow and prosper. Business owners must have a plan or strategy to generate ongoing sales and build a loyal customer base.

Product/Service Pricing

The price a business sets for owner products or services is critical to the success of your business. A practical approach is to consider what *you* would pay for your own product or service. You have already determined that there is value in what you plan to provide to your customers, now make it affordable for them and profitable for you.

There are two ways to determine the price.

1. Take actual costs and add your desired level of profit. This is the "cost plus" pricing method often used when little competition exists.

2. Look at what your competition charges and develop your prices to reflect how and where you want your products positioned and perceived in the marketplace. Do you want to have the lowest prices? Do you want to be known as providing *premium quality* products or services? Your customers' expectations will be based on your pricing structure. This is generally "the price the market can bear" or the maximum price your customers will pay.

Somewhere between your cost and "the price the market will bear" is the right price for your product or service. Once you understand your costs and your maximum price, you can make the best decision about how to price your product or service. Always keep in mind that current market trends and economic factors may dictate a change in the pricing strategy. (Small Business Facts)

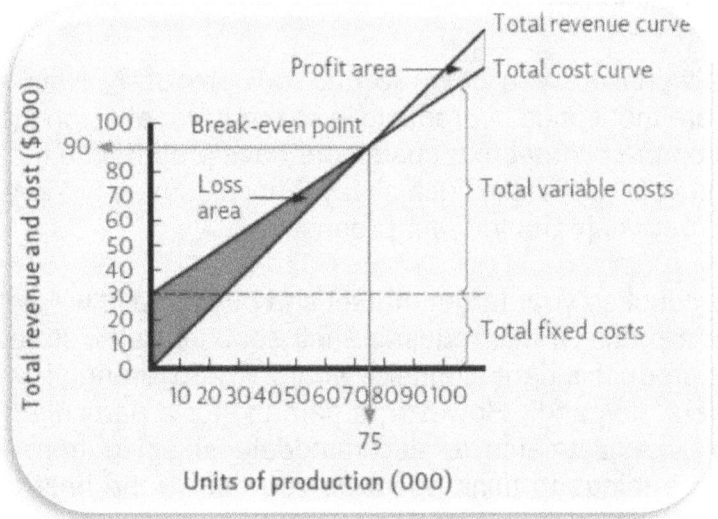

State Your Price Activity

When you conducted your research, you discovered different prices for products or services similar to yours. Write as many examples of these prices and then select the best price for the value of that product. Would you charge the same price? Why or why not? What makes your product unique and would you be willing to pay that price?

Product/Service	Price	Good value y/n

Product/Service Positioning

Now where in the world are you going to put your product? How will you store your inventory? There are thousands of products in so many varieties on the shelves, featured in magazines and on the internet that customers have a hard time making choices. You will need to position your product in such a way that customers will see it and want to buy it. The idea is to create demand for your product.

Positioning your product so your target market can purchase it, will get the desired sales you need to make a profit. If this requires shelf space in retail stores, then most likely your competition's product is right alongside yours. Keep enough inventories in stock to meet your customers' demand. However, if demand for a particular item increases, be sure to make timely adjustments to accommodate shipping from the warehouse or manufacturer. Some things to think about as you decide the best positioning for your product are:

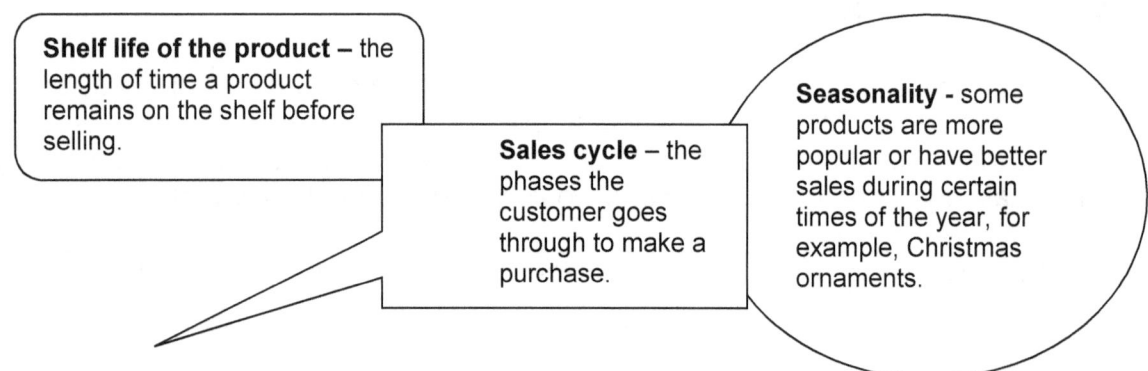

Shelf life of the product – the length of time a product remains on the shelf before selling.

Sales cycle – the phases the customer goes through to make a purchase.

Seasonality - some products are more popular or have better sales during certain times of the year, for example, Christmas ornaments.

Think about it. Some products may seem out of place as you examine the shelves in stores. Observe how the products are presented to catch the eyes of shoppers. Why do some products capture more attention than others? At the checkout, sometimes call the point-of-purchase, there are products readily available for last minute purchases.

Explain how positioning your product will get the sales activity you want.

_____

_____

_____

_____

_____

_____

Promoting and Selling

Now that you have your product/service and have set your price, how will your customers find you? Do not expect them to come crashing through your door if you have not proactively communicated your business and the benefits of your products and services. Promoting and selling create awareness for your products or services among your target market, providing messages or incentives that motivate the consumer to purchase your product. Here is your opportunity to persuade the customer that you have the right *product*, at the right *place*, for the right *price*. This is also the best way to develop brand awareness for your business or product. Associating your business name, term, sign or symbol with your product or service can leave memorable impressions on your customers especially when it generates repeat sales. Customers' loyalty to brand items with good reputations is a valuable asset.

There are three basic promotional objectives used to get a customers' attention.

- Inform – Announces the availability of and develop initial demand for a product
- Persuasive – Develop a demand for a product or service
- Remind – Reinforces previous promotional activity

There are also three avenues for promoting and selling you product or service:

- **Mass Selling**
  Mass selling involves communicating and selling to a large number of potential customers at the same time. Most well-known companies use this form of selling to distribute their products or services. It includes the use of media like magazines, newspapers, radio and TV, signs and direct mail as well as the Internet. This is a great way to build brand loyalty and get repeat sales or referrals.

- **Personal Selling**
  Personal selling is direct communication between sellers and potential customers. One of the most recognized companies that use this type very successfully is Avon.

- **Sales promotion**
  Sales promotion refers to any promotional activities beyond the advertising, public relations and personal selling arena. Sales promotion efforts are designed to get faster results.

Example 1.3 Cookie Company Promotion

The promotional plan includes initial efforts by the owners to get the cookies to decision makers in local restaurants, supermarkets, bakery shops and coffee shops. The plan will include budgeted public relations materials for communications, mostly flyers and brochures. With the development of the website, the products will be promoted with special incentives to buy more items.

Financial Plan and Forecast Analysis

Your financial plan is one of the key factors for the success of your business. It provides the financial picture by which the investors and banks will base their funding decisions. In addition, a statement of the company's financial needs, this plan must insure that the business is always liquid and ultimately profitable. Since the sales and earnings projections in the business plan are based on expectations, the financial plan has to be revised regularly so that discrepancies can be uncovered and resolved. (Small Business Facts)

Remember that the more research and information you have gleaned, the better the estimates could be for the financial plan. The inputs for your financial plan are based on size and market segments in the industry category your venture fall within. If you are opening in a location other than your home, look at all costs associated with build-outs, equipment and furniture purchases, supplies, insurance and other estimates based on the business environment.

Lenders, investors and other potential funding sources will carefully examine your financial plan. Therefore, it may be wise to solicit assistance from your business network to review these figures before submitting the business plan for funding. Dot every "i" and cross every "t" to ensure confidence that you have exercised due diligence and demonstrated commitment to success.

These figures include the initial capital investment that the owner(s) have put into the startup of the business. This action shows investors and bankers how serious you are in getting the business started or if the financial plan is for growing the business, the effort is further shown in your commitment.

Start-up Capital Budget

In the previous section, you reviewed your financial picture and determined where and how to obtain the capital needed to start your business. With money in hand, now you must determine how best to allocate those dollars to cover the cost of operating the business.

The initial amount of money needed at startup always challenges new business owners. As you plan your start-up capital budget, think carefully how much money should be allocated to each line item.

These are some legal requirements for your start-up business. You must comply with federal, state and local regulations. Include these in your budget.

Licenses, permits and certificates – as required by your locality and profession.
Insurance coverage – protects you and your venture in case of accidents, law suits, disasters, etc. Tax Identification Number (TIN), Federal Employee Identification Number (FEIN) or Social Security Number (SSN) – Every business venture must comply with federal, state and local tax laws. If you are operating as a sole proprietor, you can use your SSN. Otherwise, you can obtain a TIN or FEIN from the Internal Revenue Service (IRS).

Here is a sample budget from The Cookie Store, LLC. Note: Always add 20% unexpected costs to the first two or three years of expenses.

Start-up Capital Budget

The Cookie Store, LLC

Example 1.4

Fixtures & equipment	20,000
Decorating & remodeling	5,000
Installation of fixtures & equipment	3,500
Starting inventory	4,000
Deposits with public utilities	275
Legal & other professional fees	500
License and permits	300
Promotion/Advertising	800
Consulting & software	400
Cash	10,000
Subtotal	44,775
Monthly Expenses	
Salary of owner/manager	1,200
Other salaries/wages	1,200
Rent	875
Advertising	500

Supplies	3,000
Telephone	150
Taxes	400
Legal & other professional fees	250
Miscellaneous	1,000
Subtotal	8,575
Total	**53350**

Start-up Capital Budget

Use the table below to plan your start-up budget. Be sure to change the line items in the left column, to correspond with your business needs as you see fit.

Fixtures & equipment	
Decorating & remodeling	
Installation of fixtures & equipment	
Starting inventory	
Deposits with public utilities	
Legal & other professional fees	
License and permits	
Promotion/Advertising	
Consulting & software	
Cash	
Subtotal	
Monthly Expenses	
Salary of owner/manager	
Other salaries/wages	
Rent	
Advertising	
Supplies	
Telephone	
Taxes	
Legal & other professional fees	
Miscellaneous	
Subtotal	
Total	

Cash Flow 12-Month Forecast Statement

The cash flow statement is a monthly forecast that shows your beginning cash, cash receipts, cash disbursements and ending cash balance. Where your money is spent and how much cash you have on hand each month, are essential to operating in the "black" or with a positive cash flow. Otherwise, you may find yourself in the "red" or operating with a negative cash flow.

Keep your balance sheet close and review it monthly to get the information needed to prepare your cash flow statement. Look at the ending cash balance, add the cash receipts and subtract the disbursements or expenses. This figure is your net cash flow. Careful monitoring of this statement will help you stay on track and leave little to chance. If you use an accountant for your business, always review the statements and never assume someone else is accountable for such a crucial part of your business.

Here is a sample 6-month statement for you to review.

Example 1.5

	Month 1	Month 2	Month 3	Month 4	Month 5	Month 6
Beginning Cash	15,000	11,750	3,500	50	-1,650	100
Cash receipts						
Sales	4,400	3,000	2,900	7,000	10,000	12,000
Collections	3,300	1,200	4,500	1,500	2,000	1,800
Total cash receipts	**7,700**	**4,200**	**7,400**	**8,500**	**12,000**	**13,800**
Cash disbursements						
Salaries	6,000	6,000	6,000	6,000	6,000	6,000
Payroll Expenses	1,500	1,500	1,500	1,500	1,500	1,500
Purchases	1,000	2,500	900	250	300	1,200
Rent	2,200	2,200	2,200	2,200	2,200	2,500
Telephone	250	250	250	250	250	275
	10,950	12,450	10,850	10,200	10,250	11,475
Ending Cash Balance	11,750	3,500	50	-1,650	100	2,425

Key Financial 3-5 Year Forecasts

Income Statement

The income statement reports results of your company's financial health for a specified period of time, usually a month, quarter, or year. The income statement shows revenue, expenses and the excess of revenue over expense, known as net profit, sometimes referred to as net income. If expenses exceed revenues the income statement will show a net loss. The income statement is important because the success of the business is largely measured on its ability to generate a profit. This income statement is also referred to as the profit and loss statement.

A sample income projection statement followed by the profit and loss statement for The Cookie Store, LLC for one year are below. This projection is typically performed for the first five years. Make your projections in the blank samples below.

The Cookie Store, LLC - Income Projection statement
Example 1.6

Income Category	Oct	Nov	Dec	Jan	Feb	Mar	Apr	May	Jun	Jul	Aug	Sep	Year 1
Sweet Potato Cookies	1000	2000	3000	4000	4000	3000	3000	3000	2000	2000	3000	3000	33000
Sweet Potato Spread	400	403	407	410	413	417	420	423	427	430	433	437	5020
Sweet Potato Muffins	800	807	813	820	827	833	840	847	853	860	867	873	10040
Total Income	2200	3210	4220	5230	5240	4250	4260	4270	3280	3290	4300	4310	48060

Profit and Loss statement
Example 1.7

Column1	Oct	Nov	Dec	Jan	Feb	Mar	Apr	May	Jun	Jul	Aug	Sep	Year 1
Income	2200	3210	4220	5230	5240	4250	4260	4270	3280	3290	4300	4310	48060
Gross profit	2200	3210	4220	5230	5240	4250	4260	4270	3280	3290	4300	4310	48060
Operating expenses:													
Rent	500	500	500	1500	1500	1500	1500	1500	1500	1500	1500	1500	15000
Equipment	1000	1000	1000	1000	1000	1000	1000	1000	1000	1000	1000	1000	12000
Electricity	250	250	250	250	250	250	250	250	250	250	250	250	3000
Telephone	75	75	75	75	75	75	75	75	75	75	75	75	900
Raw Materials	367	369	370	372	373	375	376	378	379	381	382	384	4506
Amortization	36	36	36	36	36	36	36	36	36	36	36	36	432
Depreciation	123	123	123	123	123	123	123	123	123	123	123	123	1476
Total operating expenses	2351	2353	2354	3356	3357	3359	3360	3362	3363	3365	3366	3368	37314
Operating income	-151	857	1866	1874	1883	891	900	908	-83	-75	934	942	10746
Net income	-151	857	1866	1874	1883	891	900	908	-83	-75	934	942	10746

Income Projection Activity

Income Category	Oct	Nov	Dec	Jan	Feb	Mar	Apr	May	Jun	Jul	Aug	Sep	Year 1
Product 1													
Product 2													
Product 3													
Total Income													

Profit and Loss statement Activity

Column1	Oct	Nov	Dec	Jan	Feb	Mar	Apr	May	Jun	Jul	Aug	Sep	Year 1
Income													
Gross profit													
Operating expenses:													
Rent													
Equipment													
Electricity													
Telephone													
Raw Materials													
Amortization													
Depreciation													
Total operating expenses													
Operating income													
Net income													

Balance Sheet

The balance sheet is a listing of the assets, liabilities and owners' equity of your business. It is a snapshot of the state of your business on a given day, usually the end of the month or end of the fiscal year.

- **Assets** are anything of value (cash, accounts receivables, inventory, etc.) owned by the company.
- **Liabilities** are those items that are owed by the company, such as debts, accounts payable and expenses that must be paid in 12 months.
- **Owners' equity** is the owners' share of the financing of the assets, usually in the form of stocks.

The snapshot reflects all transactions that have affected your company since its inception. The balance sheet includes assets you have purchased (until sold), debts incurred (until paid), and any earnings you have retained. The balance sheet is a cumulative record of your business' financial performance. The following equation must be true in your balance sheet:

Total assets = Total liabilities + Owners' equity

Example 1.8

The Cookie Store, LLC

	Oct	Nov	Dec	Jan	Feb	Mar	Apr	May	Jun	Jul	Aug	Sep	Year 1
Assets:													
Current assets:													
Cash	13358	14374	16399	18432	20474	21524	22583	23650	23726	23810	24903	26004	26004
Inventory	3000	3000	3000	3000	3000	3000	3000	3000	3000	3000	3000	3000	3000
Total current assets	16358	17374	19399	21432	23474	24524	25583	26650	26726	26810	27903	29004	29004
Fixed assets (net)	7377	7255	7132	7010	6887	6764	6642	6519	6396	6274	6151	6029	6029
Other assets (net)	6114	6078	6043	6007	5971	5935	5899	5863	5828	5792	5756	5720	5720
Total assets	29849	30707	32574	34449	36332	37223	38124	39032	38950	38876	39810	40753	40753
Liabilities and equity:													
Current liabilities:													
Accrued liabilities	5000	5000	5000	5000	5000	5000	5000	5000	5000	5000	5000	5000	5000
Total current liabilities	5000	5000	5000	5000	5000	5000	5000	5000	5000	5000	5000	5000	5000
Total liabilities	5000	5000	5000	5000	5000	5000	5000	5000	5000	5000	5000	5000	5000
Equity	24849	25707	27574	29449	31332	32223	33124	34032	33950	33876	34810	35753	35753
Total liabilities and equity	29849	30707	32574	34449	36332	37223	38124	39032	38950	38876	39810	40753	40753

Cash Flow Statement

Now take the time to develop your cash flow statement. Use the blank form below to list your items for projecting your cash flow. Expand the chart to include as many items as needed to get a clear picture of the month.

Example 1.9

	Month 1	Month 2	Month 3	Month 4	Month 5	Month 6
Beginning Cash						
Cash receipts						
Sales						
Collections						
Total cash receipts						
Cash disbursements						
Salaries						
Payroll Expenses						
Purchases						
Rent						
Telephone						
Ending Cash Balance						

Break-even Analysis

A break-even analysis tells the business owner the amount of revenue needed to cover the cost of doing business. Sometimes called a breakeven point, this is the place in your operating budget where income from your total sales <u>must</u> equal total business expenses. Simply put, this is the point at which you neither make nor lose money in producing a product or delivering a service. If the break-even point is not achieved, your business is not bringing in enough cash to support operations and eventually the business will run out of money.

Before deciding on a fair price for a product or service, business owners must first determine their cost. Once you have identified costs, you can determine your break-even point. For example, you would be at the break-even point if it cost you $100 to produce a product that sells for $100.

To begin your break-even analysis, first add the fixed costs and determine what your variable costs are for different production volumes.

- Fixed costs, sometimes referred to as overhead, are expenses that do not vary according to production amounts - such as rent for office space (and storage space if you store inventory), office equipment (telephones, faxes, computers), insurance, and utilities.
- Variable costs are expenses that do vary with the amount of service provided or goods produced. They include costs such as hourly pay for a contractor on a specific project, and raw materials. Some variable costs don't depend specifically on the number of products produced but are still variable, such as advertising or promotion expenses.

You must know the cost of your overhead (fixed costs) as well as the incremental cost-per-unit (variable costs) before you can determine your break-even point. (Small Business Facts)

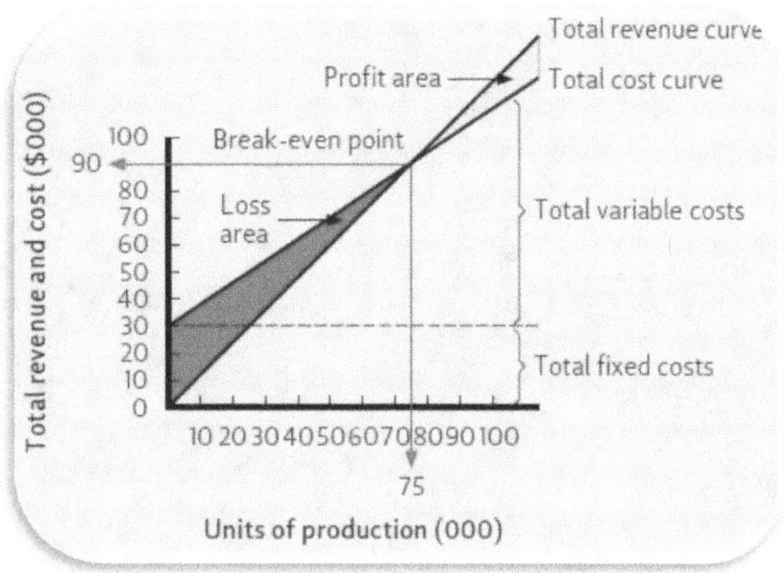

Example 1.10
Break-even Analysis

A break-even analysis is used by all businesses regardless of the service or product they provide. For example, a retail businesses' break-even point is when sales equals the cost of goods, plus operating expenses. Review the equation below, substituting actual costs to determine your break-even point.

$$S = FC + VC$$

S = sales in dollars

FC = fixed costs or operating expenses

VC = variable costs or cost of goods.

SECTION IV

PERSISTENCE
IS
KEY

Implementing Your Business Plan

WHEW! You are almost there. Do you feel a great sense of accomplishment at this point in your workbook? You have done a lot work and it will pay off. You have your road map and are ready to proceed through the next green light.

A few things you may want to consider at this point.

Re-read your plan and have a trusted associate proofread it too before meeting with the investors or bank.

Start networking with other small business owners to stay motivated. You will learn much from others and they can learn from you.

Consider building a website for your business as soon as possible. You want your potential customers to see what you can do for them.

Make sure you have the right technology to conduct business.

Keep moving forward. There will be some glitches and rocky road ahead. However, just like this workbook, you will get through it.

Step back from your plan for a few days to give yourself some 'breathing space' to clear your mind and gain clarity about your new venture.

Ask a teenager to read your plan to see if he/she understands it or if it is missing something.

Be patient! You have already decided to work for this so it is worth the effort you put into it.

Here is a suggested 'to do' list for implementing your business plan. These things can be accomplished in less than 30 days.

1. Set up your office.
2. Establish your legal entity.
3. Get the business license and/or certificate to operate in your locality.
4. Register your business with your state.
5. Create a separate business bank account.
6. Get a federal tax identification number.
7. Obtain insurance.
8. Order your supplies, inventory, business cards and forms.
9. Build your website.
10. Hire any necessary employees.

Evaluating Key Success Factors

In Section I, you identified the Key Success Factors (KSFs) for your business. These are the benchmarks by which you defined and measured whether or not your business met the desired goals. Now that you have implemented your business, revisit your KSFs regularly throughout the implementation process. Evaluate each factor with an honest assessment, identifying activities that were performed well and those that were not.

Develop recommendations for corrective action where needed with a deadline for the action to be completed. Leverage KSFs with positive results by, seeking additional ways for the company to benefit from meeting the goal. Never make the mistake of thinking that you have "arrived" and there is nothing in your business that can be improved. Once you begin to think like that, you are destined to be blindsided by your competitors and your customers will soon be theirs.

Constantly monitoring your KSFs will tell you when to move ahead, go back or change directions in your business growth.

Evaluating Your Key Success Factors

KEY SUCCESS FACTOR	Goals Met Y/N?	Recommendation By when?

Ready, Set, Go!

Congratulations, you did it! You proved that you had the *right stuff* and now are poised to grow a successful, profitable business. While your adventure may not have been smooth all the time, you persevered and reached your goal.

Going forward, use this workbook as a resource. Refer to it regularly as you explore opportunities for continued growth and as you modify your business plan to respond to economic and market changes.

Most of all make sure that you are enjoying what you do. Challenge yourself to keep alive the passion that you felt from the start. Research and develop new ways to enhance your product or augment your service. In doing so, you will always be ahead of the competition.

GODSPEED! May you and your business be blessed!

Suggested Resources

http://www.sba.gov

http://www.smallbusinessfacts.com

www.entrepreneur.com

www.startupbiz.com

http://online.wsj.com/public/page/news-small-business-marketing.html

www.fastcompany.com

Business Plan Template

I.   Cover Sheet

II.   Executive Summary

III.   General Company Description

IV.   Products and Services

V.   Marketing Plan

VI.   Operational Plan

VII.   Management and Organization

VIII. Financial Strategy

IX.   Appendix

Business Plan Template

Your Company Name

Your Street Address
City State Zip
2021111111
user@company.com
www.domain.com

Entrepreneurship 101: The NEW Reality of Business Ownership 74

Business Plan Template

Table of Contents

Executive Summary

Business Description and Vision

Definition of the Market

Description of the Products and Services

Organization and Management

Marketing and Sales Strategy

Financial Management

Appendices

This section should include as attachments:

- Company brochures
- Resumes of key employees
- List of business equipment
- Copies of press articles and advertisements (if available)
- Pictures of your business location and products (optional)
- Information supporting the growth of your industry and/or products (optional)

In memory of Natalynn B. Roman.  Together, we can find a cure.

About the Author

Vanessa Womack Easter, MBA

Vanessa Womack Easter has a diverse background in training and professional development, entrepreneurship, higher education instruction, human resources, nonprofit, and leadership development. She has been a faculty member at the University of Phoenix Richmond – Virginia Beach campus for 10 years where she has been a lead faculty area chair in the School of Business and mentor to new faculty.

Before accepting a full time position with a state Primary Care Association in 2013, she successfully worked for nearly 20 years as a 'solopreneur' and consultant. Vanessa's community engagement and leadership roles included being president of the board of directors of Virginia Heroes Incorporated (a middle school mentoring program founded by Arthur Ashe) and a former advisory council member for the Virginia Commonwealth University - Grace E. Harris Leadership Institute Minority Political Leadership Institute (GEHLI – MPLI) and Initiatives of Change/ Hope in the Cities.

Vanessa received her undergraduate degree from CUNY/Baruch College and MBA from Averett University. She is a graduate of Leadership Metro Richmond (LQ 2006). She has facilitated community dialogue and presented at national conferences such as Teach for America and Society of Government Meeting Professionals. Vanessa is a BoardSource Certified Governance Trainer.

She is the author of *'Paint the Sky Purple'* (2010) and co-author with other international women's voices in '*The Female CEO: Pearls, Power & Passion'* (August 2014). She hosted conversations on her former radio show *'On Track with Vanessa Womack'* which also has videos posted on YouTube.

Contact information:
vanessawomack@gmail.com

http://www.linkedin.com/in/vanessawomackeastermba

804.307.7102

www.ingramcontent.com/pod-product-compliance
Lightning Source LLC
Chambersburg PA
CBHW080719190526
45169CB00006B/2436